MW01289379

SEX

after

60

New Condensed Edition!

★★★★★

This is a BLANK GAG BOOK eluding to the fact that you have no sex life after turning sixty! Feel free to use this as a notebook in the future as we've left plenty of space for your thoughts! More titles are available at www.BlankGagBooks.com. All testimonials and content are fake and intended for entertainment purposes only. Any resemblance to the names, faces, characters or content is purely coincidental. Rich Ferguson Entertainment or its partners are not liable for any misuse of this book. You gift this at your own risk of rejection, humiliation, danger or injury. However, if you find that you are the hit of the party or make lots of new friends then we take full credit and will accept cash or credit donations!

THEICEBREAKER.COM

Written and Designed by Rich Ferguson, AKA "The Ice Breaker" Rich Ferguson is an award winning magician and entrepreneur. For entertainment booking for special events, please visit Rich's official site at www.TheIceBreaker.com

For more Blank Gag Book titles, go to www.BlankGagBooks.com

SEX after 60

SEX after 60

SEX after 60

SEX after 60

SEX after 60

SEX after 60

SEX after 60

SEX after 60

SEX after 60

SEX after 60

SEX after 60

SEX after 60

SEX after 60

SEX after 60

SEX after 60

SEX after 60

SEX after 60

SEX after 60

SEX after 60

SEX after 60

SEX after 60

SEX after 60

SEX after 60

SEX after 60

SEX after 60

SEX after 60

SEX after 60

SEX after 60

SEX after 60

SEX after 60

SEX after 60

SEX after 60

SEX after 60

SEX after 60

SEX after 60

SEX after 60

SEX after 60

SEX after 60

SEX after 60

SEX after 60

SEX after 60

SEX after 60

SEX after 60

SEX after 60

SEX after 60

SEX after 60

SEX after 60

SEX after 60

SEX after 60

SEX after 60

SEX after 60

SEX after 60

SEX after 60

SEX after 60

SEX after 60

SEX after 60

SEX after 60

SEX after 60

SEX after 60

SEX after 60

SEX after 60

SEX after 60

SEX after 60

SEX after 60

SEX after 60

SEX after 60

SEX after 60

SEX after 60

SEX after 60

SEX after 60

SEX after 60

SEX after 60

SEX after 60

SEX after 60

SEX after 60

SEX after 60

SEX after 60

SEX after 60

SEX after 60

SEX after 60

SEX after 60

SEX after 60

More titles available at
BlankGagBooks.com